built and broken

Sanjita Jain

BookLeaf
Publishing

India | USA | UK

Presentation by *BookLeaf Publishing*

Web: www.bookleafpub.com

E-mail: info@bookleafpub.com

ISBN: 9789357444484

First edition 2021

DEDICATION

This collection is dedicated to:

1. The commenters on my early fiction, who encouraged me through comma splices and run-on sentences to continue creating and never stop. Without you, I never would've written enough to be good at what I do

2. My friends and family, who supplied me with the best and the worst of their STEM related fields to exploit for my own uses. To Crow and Darius, thank you for your encouragement, and for collecting the rains of my brainstorms into usable little buckets.

3. Most of all, my family: my parents set me loose in a library every single time I asked and read poetry with no idea of what an enjoyment even is, and if not for you, I would still be struggling with tenses on homework assignments.

rocket ships

you were the stars in the skies
i flew too close and burned my eyes
and now i hide the tears
in the rain with the pain and the fear
you kept shining
found new pilots, a new silver lining

and i stayed grounded
crash landed
a crater
a memorial of my own making

adrenaline, adrenaline through my veins,
clear the clouds, find what remains
burn our fuel, let it all drain
fly this heart till we go insane

give me your attention, give me your time
give me your love, even if loving's a crime
because baby, starships were meant to fly
so can we maybe give this one more try

i am the earth by the sea
you are the wind, sweet ocean breeze
flying fast and flying free
left me on lock and stole the keys
you're still flying
past the sunrise, through that golden lighting

and i'm still grounded
crash landed
a gravestone
a memorial of my own making

adrenaline, adrenaline through my veins,
clear the clouds, find what remains
burn our fuel, let it all drain
fly this heart till we go insane

give me your attention, give me your time
give me your love, even if loving's a crime
because baby, starships were meant to fly
so can we maybe give this one more try

because baby, starships were meant to fly
so can we maybe give this one last try

decay

I don't believe you when you promise you'll stay
Where were you when I needed you just
yesterday
Told me you love me, told me that you would
care,
That I stole your breath, won your heart, I don't
have to share

Now I'm missing you, messing with you, what
do I do?
I'm left behind again 'cause you think we're
through
Tell me leave you alone, I should've known, too
good to be true
I don't remember who I used to be before you

I won't ask you to stay
Won't ask you to fix this mess
Let our love decay
Let you walk away, walk away
Downplay, downplay, downplay
You'll take your sanity, I'll take on your stress

I wish what I say would be heard, would be
seen
You ignore my words, turn around, talk right
over me
Make these promises I want to believe
But I'm not naive, I know you'll leave, break the
heart on my sleeve

Now I'm stuck here alone, this broken throne,
will I have grown?
I'll just forgive it all, make your pain my own
Swallow back blood and bone, couldn't have
known, the colors you've shown
I'm sick and tired of this broken home

Should I ask you to stay?
Ask you to fix this mess
Or let our love decay
Can I walk away, walk away
Downplay, downplay, downplay
The way you hurt me, the pain and the stress

I made you my priority
I made you my team
I made you my promises
I made you my dream

I made you important
I made you my heart
You took it all in hand
You tore it apart

I won't ask you to stay
Won't ask you to fix this mess
Let our love decay
Let you walk away, walk away
Downplay, downplay, downplay
Pick up the pieces now, let go of the stress

I'm picking up my pieces now, letting go of
distress

celestial

the heavens burst open
in a moment of pain, in a shower of fear
but i opened my eyes
and you were right here

the planets collided
and nothing was left, just a broken mess
but i opened my heart
i have no regrets

in the wasteland created
in destruction and hatred
the stars, they waited
and angel, we were fated

you're the iron in my veins
you're the love that remains
you're kindness and trust
angel, you are stardust

give me your heart and I'll do the same
I'll give you my time and I'll take your name
kiss by the fire and kiss by the flames
we'll fall and fly and let go of our shame

give me the world I want to roam
I'll see it all and make my throne
with forests tall and ocean foam
we'll build and bridge and make our home

sewing kit

our nights end in
bandaids and broken hearts
long days and we fall apart
into sketchy blueprints, euphoric sin
balming soup for our too-thin skin

we are torn apart and sewn back together
pinned aground by a needle's tether

our days start instead
tracing patterns and chalking lines
starting over just to burn our time
stitch our hearts with golden thread
so wax wings shed blood instead

timer

sand like possibility in the palm of my hand
opportunities, potential,
just slipping through
my own clumsy
fingertips.
gone.

but my broken heart
is made of trust
not so easily ground to dust
nonplussed I'll readjust
build a home from bloody rust

because
in my hands
I hold my hopes
of growing up again
and molding clay to find
all I can build and all I can be
I am more than who I used to be

black hole

say there were words here
words I meant to write
words that made you feel things
evocative and bright

say there were words here
words I wrote with weight
words that caught your heart up
dangled you like bait

say there were words here
words I should've said
words that could've bridged the gap
between what's left for dead

say there were words here
words I still don't have
words that made things easier
to cut this space in half

say there were words here
words I wouldn't know
words that explained somehow
that I don't want you to go

say there were words here
words I know aren't wrong
words that told you how I felt
how I'd felt all along

say there were words here
words I could hold tight
words that said I'm not alone
and kept me warm at night

say there were words here
words that I won't say
words like, you hurt me first
then led me astray

say there was love here
love I build myself
love that carries me forward
towards a new life's breath

quantum entanglement

you scrawl a memoir in my **hand**
for you I'd reach my **hand** across
time & space, **hand** you the world
in your **hand** to hold next to mine
hand it to me, I've held myself **back**

back again and I'm here to **stay**
so go **back** to the days when our
words came **back** to us in ways
we wish we'd taken **back** but
we've only got mistakes to **back**

if we have forever, promise you'll **stay**
say you'll find our page, **stay** here
you could wait, **stay** your reckless rebel
heart, **stay** because you want to
stay just because I asked you **today**

today is all we've got to **hold**
I know **today** is getting old
who knows if **today** is all that
we meant for it to be **today**, but
the stars are taking you away **today**

I've got nothing left now to **hold**
so offer your hand to **hold** onto
or will I just **hold** you back
if you **hold** onto what we made
hold onto what was built and broken

string theory

tangled, spoken, left unopened
for a rebel heart left choking
on the words you couldn't say
couldn't find it in yourself to be brave

all our lives you stayed right here
never found a chance to fear
all the worries in my head
but here you are in my stead

waiting, watching, worry wanting
taunting, haunting, not the calming
friend I knew to keep me safe
I bet that cowardice chafes

tell me what I mean to you
tell me what is true
or smudge the ink and run away
I'll live to love another day

my love is caught in your fingertips
a web of lies built of hidden scripts
there's a love there on your lips
but our time is over now: snip snip

toolbox

pandora's box has burst open:
these monsters of ours to rope in

chop with scissors, cut with knives
we're building up our hope tonight

pin this greed in place, hammer it in,
toss our cruelty into the bin

patchwork wood, hungry glue
take my hand, I'll work with you

this envy is a driver of screws
but we can wrench out the truth

drill this vice out of our hearts
warm our hands down by the hearth

clamp down on disease tonight
level our feelings, keep them bright

polish smooth your practiced thought
watch the edges of what you saw

one last thing left to unpack
our hope to triumph, back to back

ruler

you might've been a good man
but you wouldn't be the man for me,
you've loved me despite everything you've
known
there's nothing left to change or write
about our precious history,
you've made mistakes and I know that you've
grown
so tell me that you'll be alone
that no one sees what you have shown
like valor and resolve on your throne
and think of all the ways you've sown
kindness in the land you own,
and know that I will greet you coming home

wordsmith

i don't always know the right words to say
but i know that you always make my day

by the way that your hand fits right into mine
by the way that your smile shimmers and shines
by the way that you always do what you want
by the way that i get to be your confidante
by the way that you are more than you seem
by the way that you know just what i mean

so it's okay that i don't quite know what to say
i just know that i have to try today
Will you come home with me to stay?

molecular

attraction

actually: math is humanities.
Science is humanities. what is science if not: a
story about two molecules who
    fell in love, who fought
the existence of energy
itself
to be together?
Who paid the price for the love they carried?
who were so-drawn-to each other
among millions of others
that they could not help but to touch?
what is math if not:
the adding of a baby in your life, the
f r a c t i o n a t i o n
of a friend group,
the division
        of labor?
actually: these are all the same.
They are all made of love.

spatial recognition

Where am i? Where have you gone?
how can i find myself within this place
without you holding on?

you tell me there is space here
between us, where we stood in embrace
now standing so unclear

i reach out to find you away
ahead of me, already free, not to be chased
but the race is underway

we have something missing there
all the many ways we met have been erased
into blankness we can't share

the rift here is a fission
a boundary meant for my fingers to trace
over spatial recognition

spatial attraction

you hold yourself apart from me
keep a distance we don't share
i don't care

you make yourself small as can be
and wilt under their stare
i don't care

you tense your body ready to flee
and jump at every scare
i don't care

i recognize you
and the person that you are to me
i know the space between us
my loving enemy
boundaries

so keep yourself away
if it keeps you safe and here to stay
this space becomes a canvas we share
painted over with color and light and
all the things we cannot bear

my spatial recognition
is permission, no condition
you can hold yourself as far as you want to
and i will be right here for you
i will keep on loving you
here, or there, or anywhere

i don't care

01110000

01100001

01110000

01100001

you and me
are like binary
infinite possibilities
of everything we can be

bits strung neatly in a queue
build the world through
system base two
me and you

trust fx

breathe in, breathe out
watch her heartrate fill with doubt
pitter patter, faster, faster
this is already disaster

subject: human 713
She doesn't trust me.
because i am metal scraps
unalive, perhaps

keep my distance, stay aside
turn my rotors, shorten strides
i will be a safe robot
trustworthy: as i was wrought

The human (713) is tired.
she has not slept; i am wired
to help her. i track her quiet sobs
get ready to do my job

my motors hum, tilted down
i offer sympathetic sounds
bring warm blankets, offer tea
still she does not speak to me

human 713 shrieks.
my detectors sense a pique
of pressure and noise;
i will stay poised

I have been taught about grief.
despite her current disbelief,
subject human 713 will learn
my programming fakes concern

trust me, follow through
eat the fruits i bring to you
lean in close, whisper near
all your secrets, all your fears

for subject 713, this
is a matter of bliss.
my trust function
will ensure capitulation.

trust function, trust fix
my code has done the trick
i extract her fast devotion
by mocking her human emotions

gravity

the clouds are ashen and the skies are gray
we've forgotten what it's like when
the falling rain brings joy to play
you left me behind and
never, not once have
you felt for me

(read up)

proof of concept

build your story up, write your pitch
hold your tongue, don't stutter, not a twitch
offer prototypes like godly sacrifice
ready to build? oh, darling, take my advice

nothing breaks beneath pinpricked fingertips
practice confidence with executive scripts
take that hope of yours and make it smoke
no one invests in dreams if it'll get broke

proof of
completion

your theory is just meant to be
a promise of your anguished plea
a prototype is in your hands
but don't you want to build a brand?

build some more, build a store,
build a market out of whores
lust for money, precious sum
every milked out drop or crumb

proof of capital

settle down in that tarnished crown of coins
build an empire of employees, begin to enjoin
work fast, work harder, send a patent to the
martyr
trade favors, learn to barter, better draft a
damning charter

your concept's good enough but good enough is
just beginning
own the market that you started, don't you wish
you weren't sinning?
it's a game, it's a ruse, it's a contest that you
lose,
make your product, start to shmooze, build
enough until you bruise

recombinant dna

read me to my very base
dna polymerase
a library of nucleotides
leave nothing i can hide

this twisting turning helix
unbinds into the prefix
of duplicitous division
fundamental fragmentation

our dna entwines
builds a twisting turning spine
of chimeric combination
a social celebration

for we are humans at our core
there is nothing we want more
than to find the people of our heart
and never spend our days apart